CO

CW00394160

HOW MUCH PENSION DO YOU NEED?   2

SECTION 1: YOUR PENSION CHOICES   4

If you work for an employer   4
If you are self-employed   5
If you are not in employment   5

SECTION 2: YOUR STATE PENSION   6

Basic pension   6
State Earnings Related Pension Scheme   9
Graduated pension   12
Action now   12
More information about state pensions   13

**SECTION 3: EMPLOYERS'
PENSION SCHEMES**   14

What employers' schemes offer   14
Types of employers' schemes   15
What employers' schemes cost   16
Leaving your scheme before retirement   16
Boosting your pension   17
Contracting out   18
Pros and cons of employers' pension
schemes   19
Action now   21
More information about employers'
schemes   23

**SECTION 4: PERSONAL
PENSION PLANS**   24

How personal pension plans work   24
What personal pension plans cost   25
Contracting out   26
How your money is invested   27
Buying a personal pension plan   29
What if you have a Section 226 plan?   31
Pros and cons of personal pension plans   31
Action now   32
More information about personal
pension plans   34

GLOSSARY OF PENSIONSPEAK   36

HOW MUCH PENSION DO YOU NEED?

It's likely that you belong to the state pension scheme. But this alone is very unlikely to provide you with enough retirement income to maintain a reasonable lifestyle – and may not be enough even to cover the basics of life. You will need to make extra savings for retirement.

How much income you want in retirement is largely a matter of personal choice. You are unlikely to need as much as you do while you are working and supporting a family: by the time you retire you might own your home outright with no more mortgage to pay, you probably won't be paying out any more for your children's education, you might save a fair amount through not travelling to work any more. You might be aiming for around, say, half to three-quarters of your pre-retirement income.

A companion Action Pack 'FINANCE YOUR FUTURE' is available which gives full guidance on working out how much retirement income you'll need – see p40.

But providing a decent pension at retirement age may not be enough. On average, a man retiring at the state pension age of 65 can expect to survive another 13 years; a woman retiring at 60 another 21 years. And with the age of retirement tending to drop, you could easily end up relying on your pension for 20 or 30 years. What may be enough to live on in your 60s may be quite inadequate when you are 80 or 90.

The amount you need to build up can be considerable, not just because retirement can be a big chunk of your life, but also because inflation can eat into the value of your money. The Table right shows how various rates of inflation eat into the value of £1,000 over the years.

EXAMPLE

Kevin is aged 45 and setting aside £100 a month in a pension plan. This might accumulate a fund of, say, £75,000 by the time he reaches 65, which he could expect to provide a pension of, say, £9,750 a year. That perhaps sounds a reasonable sum, but if price inflation averages just 4 per cent a year over the 20 years to his retirement, a loaf of bread costing 65p now would cost £1.42 when he retires. £9,750 would be worth only £4,450 in terms of what he could buy with it. And, of course, inflation will continue to affect his pension after retirement too.

HOW INFLATION AFFECTS THE VALUE OF YOUR MONEY

What £1,000 would be worth at different rates of inflation

Years	Average rate of inflation		
	4% a year	7% a year	10% a year
	£	£	£
1	962	935	909
2	925	873	826
3	889	816	751
4	855	763	683
5	822	713	621
10	676	508	386
15	555	362	239
20	456	258	149
25	375	184	92
30	308	131	57
35	253	94	36
40	208	67	22.
45	171	48	14
50	141	34	9
60	95	17	3

Planning your pension

It takes time to build up enough savings to provide a reasonable pension, so you should start saving as early as you can. Naturally, the longer you invest, the more you'll save, but you'll also be giving your investment a longer time in which to grow. If you start setting aside money for your pension when you are in your 30s your chances of an adequate pension will be better than if you wait until your 40s. If you start saving in your 20s, that's even better.

You might be a bit daunted by the thought of setting aside money for so many years and for a time which seems such a long way off. It can be tempting to put your retirement savings into a building society account, say, or a unit trust where you can get at your money before retirement if you need to. But resist the temptation: apart from the importance of saving for retirement, there are big tax incentives with a proper pension scheme or plan. The taxman adds to your money – you get tax relief on the money you pay in, your invested money grows tax-free, and you can take part of the proceeds of most schemes and plans as a tax-free lump sum at the time you retire.

Which sort of pension scheme or plan you can opt for depends on your work:

- if you work for a company, your employer may run a pension scheme which you can join, or you might be attracted to taking out your own personal pension plan. Either way, you might also decide to opt out of the earnings-related part of the state pension scheme

- if you're self-employed, you'll need to take out a personal pension plan, to supplement the state basic pension (you're not covered by the earnings-related part)

- if you don't have any earnings from employment or self-employment, you can't contribute to a pension scheme or plan, but there might be steps you could take to protect your state pension.

Whatever your situation, this Action Pack will guide you through the options that you face. But everyone's situation is different, and there are no easy answers when you look at your pension. So you'll need to do a bit of detective work yourself to find out the details of some of the schemes available to you, and you'll have to think about what you personally need from your pension arrangements. We strongly recommend that you get advice from pensions experts who can look at your own personal circumstances. This Pack will help you to gather the necessary information, guide you to the appropriate experts, help you to understand and weigh up the information and advice you are given, and help you to make the best choices about your pension.

YOUR PENSION CHOICES

The route maps on these pages will help you identify the choices that you face if you work for an employer, if you are self-employed, or if you are not in employment. They suggest which courses of action you should consider and tell you which parts of this Booklet deal with your particular situation.

YOUR PENSION CHOICES IF YOU WORK FOR AN EMPLOYER
[1] [2] **See Section 2, Section 3, and Section 4**

If you pay married women's reduced rate National Insurance (see p6) you may be better off switching to full rate – see p12

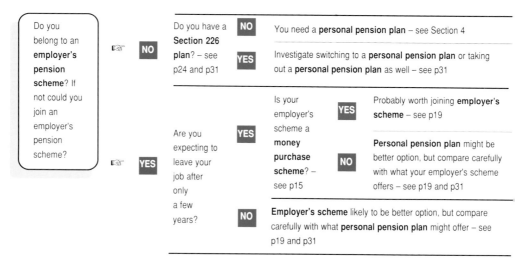

AND SHOULD YOU CONTRACT OUT OF SERPS IF YOU WORK FOR AN EMPLOYER
See p10

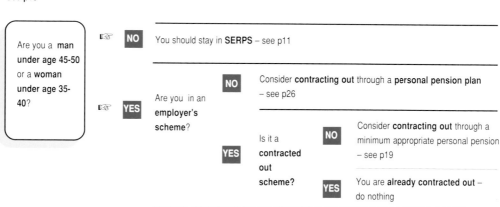

1

We recommend that you have a brief look at the relevant route maps now and read the pages referred to. Then come back and look at the maps again in more detail to check your choices before using the *Action Now* guides in each Section to take you step-by-step through the things you need to do. The *Action Now* guides will also show you how the checklists, record sheets, tables and directory in the back of the Pack can help you take the right action and keep track of your pension savings.

YOUR PENSION CHOICES IF YOU ARE SELF-EMPLOYED
[1] [3] **See Section 2 and Section 4**

If you are a married woman or widow or someone on low earnings who chooses not to pay Class 2 National Insurance (see p6). you may be better off paying contributions

Do you have a **Section 226 plan** (see p24 and p31)?

☞ **NO** You need a **personal pension plan** – see Section 4

☞ **YES** Do you want to start taking pension before age 60?

  YES Investigate switching to a **personal pension plan** or taking out a **personal pension plan** as well – see p31

  NO Carry on your **Section 226 plan** – see p31. But consider taking advantage of higher contribution limits for personal pension plans – see p26

YOUR PENSION CHOICES IF YOU ARE NOT IN EMPLOYMENT
[1] **See Section 2**

Are you caring for someone at home?

☞ **YES** Check whether you qualify for **Home Responsibilities Protection** – see p7 and p13

Are you sick, disabled, unemployed, training or pregnant?

☞ **YES** Check whether you're getting **National Insurance credits** – see p7 and p13

Are you taking a break from work or studying at college or university?

☞ **YES** Consider making **voluntary National Insurance contributions** – see p6 and p13

Boosting your pension

[1] If you've gaps in your National Insurance record in the last 6 years. consider voluntary contributions – see p6 and p12

[2] If you belong to an employer's scheme. consider making extra voluntary contributions – see p17

[3] If your contributions to Section 226 plans and personal pension plans are less than tax rules allow consider increasing payments. or taking out an additional personal pension plan – see p26

YOUR STATE PENSION

There are two main state pensions: the flat-rate basic pension and the State Earnings Related Pension Scheme (SERPS, also known as the 'additional' pension). You might also be entitled to benefits from the older graduated pension scheme.

You qualify for one or more of the state pensions by making enough National Insurance (NI) contributions of the right type; in general, more years of contributions mean more pension – up to a point. For more about National Insurance contributions, see Box below.

BASIC PENSION

Who qualifies?
Everyone working for an employer and paying Class 1 NI contributions. So, too, do the self-employed who pay Class 2 NI contributions (though any Class 4 contributions you pay don't count towards basic pension). People who volunteer to pay Class 3 NI contributions to make up gaps in their contribution record also build up baiic pension. Some married women and widows pay Class 1 NI contributions at a special married woman's reduced rate.

NATIONAL INSURANCE CONTRIBUTIONS

There are four 'Classes' of NI contributions; which Class you pay depends on your circumstances. A National Insurance contribution year is the same as a tax year: it runs from 6 April to the following 5 April.

Class 1 contributions These are paid by employees (and their employers) whose earnings exceed the Lower Earnings Limit. This Limit is set each year, and is £43 a week (£186 a month) for the11989-90 tax year. Employees pay Class 1 contributions on earnings up to the Upper Earnings Limit (£325 a week or £1,408 a month for 1989-90); employers pay Class 1 contributions on all employees' earnings without limit.

There are several different rates of Class 1 contributions. Which you pay depends on your earnings and on whether you are contracted out of SERPS.

Some married women and widows pay Class 1 contributions at a special married woman's reduced rate (this option was withdrawn from 6 April 1977 and only women who opted before then can pay this rate).

Class 2 contributions Self-employed people pay Class 2 NI contributions at a single flat rate. But if the profits from your business are below a certain limit (£2,350 in 1989-90), you can choose not to pay contributions. Some married women and widows can choose not to pay Class 2 contributions (provided they made this choice before 6 April 1977).

Class 3 contributions If you've got gaps in your NI contributions record, you can volunteer to pay Class 3 contributions. You can only make good gaps up to six years ago – so in the 1989-90 tax year, you can go back as far as 1983-84. Note that married women and widows who pay reduced Class 1 rate or no Class 2 contributions cannot use Class 3 contributions to make these up.

Class 4 contributions These are paid by the self-employed on profits between certain limits (£5,050 and £16,900 for 1989-90)

These don't count towards a basic pension (though you may get a pension based on your husband's contributions).

In some situations, you may be credited with NI contributions, without having to pay them. For example, this happens if:

- you are claiming certain state benefits, such as unemployment, maternity or sickness benefit

- you are a man within five years of state pension age and unemployed – you get credits without having to 'sign on'

- you were born after 5 April 1957 – you get credits for the years in which you had your 16th, 17th and 18th birthdays if you were still at school

- you were born after 5 April 1957 – you get credits for the years in which you are taking part in an approved training course. (This doesn't include going to university.)

If you stay at home to care for a child, or someone who's sick or elderly, you may qualify for Home Responsibilities Protection. This reduces the number of years of contributions that you need to count towards a basic pension.

Since 6 April 1975, only a full year's worth of contributions counts towards the basic pension. You can build up entitlement with a mixture of different classes of contributions in the same year – one Class 2 or 3 contribution, or one credit, is equivalent to one week's Class 1 contribution. If you have a part-year of contributions, it won't count, so it may be worth paying Class 3 contributions to make up a complete year. The Table summarises the NI contributions which count towards the state basic pension.

2

DO YOUR CONTRIBUTIONS COUNT TOWARDS BASIC PENSION?

Type of contribution	Description	Do they count towards basic pension?	How many needed for a tax year to count towards basic pension?
Class 1 (at full rate)	paid by employees except those earning below the Lower Earnings Limit	YES	contributions on earnings at least 52 times the weekly Lower Earnings Limit
Class 1 (at married reduced rate)	some married women and widows pay at an optional lower rate	NO	N/A
Class 2	paid by self-employed	YES	52 contributions
Class 3	voluntary	YES	52 contributions
Class 4	paid by self-employed earning more than a given amount	NO	N/A

Notes: The information in this Table applies from 6 April 1975, except Class 1 contributions which applies from 6 April 1978. Up to 5 April 1975, both employees (except those on low earnings) and self-employed paid NI contributions at a single rate; all these contributions are added together, then divided into 'lots' of 50 – each lot and the remaining part-lot count as a year's worth of contributions. From 6 April 1975 to 5 April 1978, Class 1 contributions on earnings of at least 50 (not 52) times the Lower Earnings Limit were enough for a year to qualify.

How much pension?

The full basic pension is £43.60 a week (£2,267.20 a year) for a single person and £69.80 (£3,629.60) for a married couple for the year 6 April 1989 to 5 April 1990. If both husband and wife qualify for a basic pension in their own right they can jointly get up to 2 x £43.60 = £87.20 a week (£4,534.40 a year). The basic pension is usually increased each year in line with inflation (measured by changes in the Retail Prices Index).

To qualify for the full pension, you must normally have paid or been credited with NI contributions for about 90 per cent of the tax years in your working life (as officially defined). For most people the length of their working life means the tax years starting with the year in which you reach age 16 and ending with the last complete year before you reach state pension age. So working life is usually 44 years if you're a woman, and 49 years if you're a man. If you were born before 5 July 1932, see below right.

EXAMPLE

Christine is a 30-year old career woman; her working life is 44 years. She began paying Class 1 contributions when she left university at 21 and expects this to continue until she retires (38 full years in all). She was at school when she reached 16 until the time she went to college so she will have contribution credits for those three years. The only gap in her contributions record is the three years she spent at university. But having paid, or been credited with, contributions for 41 years, she has achieved a contribution record equal to about 93 per cent of her working life. This would qualify her for a basic pension at the full rate.

If you have paid, or been credited with, NI contributions for less than about 90 per cent of the tax years during your working life, you may still be entitled to basic pension – but at a reduced rate. As long as you have contributions for about a quarter of your working life, you'll probably get some basic pension; if you have fewer years than that, you might not get any basic pension at all. You can use Sheet A *Basic Pension Calculator* in the back pocket of this Pack to work out how much of the basic pension you'll be entitled to.

EXAMPLE

George has a working life of 46 years (see below for how he worked this out). He looks along the top of the *Basic Pension Calculator* and finds 46 years. Then he looks down the side to find the number of years of contributions he expects to have which count towards the basic pension if he carries on paying contributions up to retirement – this comes to 39 years in his case. The figure in the Table where the working life column and contribution years row meet is 96. This means that George can expect to qualify for 96 per cent of the full state basic pension.

If you are widowed, or divorced, and have not remarried before retirement, your former husband's or wife's contributions might count towards your basic pension.

Born before 5 July 1932?

If you were born before 5 July 1932, your working life will be shorter than 44 years for a woman and 49 years for a man. Use the route map opposite.

EXAMPLE

George was born on 18 December 1927 so he uses the route map to work out the length of his working life. He answers YES to 'Were you born before 5 July 1932?'. He was paying contributions to a state scheme on 5 July 1948, so he answers YES to the next question. He had started contributing in August 1946 and contributed without a break up to 5 July 1948. So George's working life starts on 6 April 1946 and ends on 5 April 1992 – the end of the tax year in which he reaches age 64 (the last complete tax year before he reaches state pension age). This gives a working life of 46 years.

Were you born before 5 July 1932?

☞ **NO** Working life begins on 6 April of the tax year in which you reach 16 and ends on 5 April of the tax year in which you reach 64 (men) or 59 (women)

☞ **YES** Were you contributing to an old state pension scheme on 5 July 1948?

NO Working life begins on 6 April 1948. It ends on 5 April of the tax year in which you reach 64 (men) or 59 (women) [1]

YES Your working life begins on 6 April of the tax year before 1948 in which you LAST started to contribute. It ends on 5 April of the tax year in which you reach 64 (men) or 59 (women) [1] [2]

2

[1] If your working life began before 5 July 1948. you are credited with the contributions for each week from the start of your working life up to 5 July 1948

[2] For people who had been contributing to an old scheme since 6 April 1936 or earlier. working life began on 6 April 1936 and ended on 5 April of the tax year in which they reached 64 (men) or 59 (women)

STATE EARNINGS RELATED PENSION SCHEME

Who qualifies?

Only people working for an employer can build up State Earnings Related Pension Scheme (SERPS) pension. So you can't belong to SERPS during any periods when you're self-employed. You build up SERPS pension by paying Class 1 NI contributions (at the full rate). Each week that you pay contributions adds to your SERPS pension – you do not need complete years of contributions. This means that you can be building up SERPS pension even if you're not building up basic pension. But the weeks that you're not paying Class 1 contributions can reduce the SERPS pension that you get – for example, if you are unemployed or earning too little to pay NI contributions.

How much pension?

Calculating the amount of SERPS pension you will get is complicated. Happily, the Department of Social Security (DSS) will supply you with a statement of your entitlement on request – see p12. What follows is a brief explanation of how SERPS entitlement is worked out – and how the amount of pension you will get from SERPS will fall after 1998.

The amount of SERPS pension you get depends on your 'surplus earnings' in the years for which you've paid full Class 1 NI contributions. Surplus earnings are worked out as follows:

Step 1: for each year since April 1978, earnings on which you've paid Class 1 contributions at the full rate are taken; earnings above the Upper Earnings Limit are ignored

Step 2: these earnings are increased each year up to retirement in line with national average earnings

Step 3: the Lower Earnings Limit in the year of retirement is subtracted from each revalued earnings figure to leave 'surplus earnings'.

Your SERPS pension is a fraction of your total surplus earnings, the fraction depending on when you retire:

- if you retire on or before 5 April 1998, one-eightieth of each year's surplus earnings. Since there will be a maximum of 20 years' contributions by 1998, the maximum SERPS pension will be equivalent to roughly one-quarter (20 x 1/80) of your average earnings between the Lower and Upper Earnings Limits. At the current levels of the Earnings Limits, the maximum SERPS pension would be roughly £3,600 a year

- if you retire after 5 April 1998, the maximum SERPS pension will be gradually reduced over ten years, falling to a fifth of average earnings between the Lower and Upper Earnings Limit. So eventually the maximum SERPS pension would be roughly £2,900 a year at the current levels of the Earnings Limits.

After retirement, SERPS pension is increased in line with inflation (measured by changes in the Retail Prices Index). There are also rules which allow your widow to inherit part of your SERPS pension entitlement if you die before or after retirement. Your widower can inherit part of your SERPS pension but only if you are over 60 and he is over 65 at the time of your death.

EXAMPLE

Tom retired in September 1988. He had belonged to SERPS since 6 April 1984. This is how his SERPS pension was calculated:

Step 1: his earnings for each tax year that he was in SERPS (1984-85 to 1988-89) were £10,070, £11,000, £11,700, £13,500, £8,200 – all below the Upper Earnings Limit

Step 2: these earnings were revalued in line with average earnings up to the last tax year (1987-88) before he reached state pension age of 65. This gave him revalued earnings of £13,565, £13,992, £13,666, £14,675 and £8,200

Step 3: the Lower Earnings Limit when Tom reached retirement was £2,132. This was subtracted from each revalued earnings figure to leave surplus earnings of £11,433, £11,860, £11,534, £12,548 and £6,068.

Adding these together gave £53,438 and one-eightieth of this gave a yearly pension of £668 (£12.84 a week). This will be increased each year in line with changes in the Retail Price Index.

Contracting out

You may contract out of SERPS through a personal pension arrangement or through joining a contracted out employer's pension scheme. This means that you give up part of your SERPS pension and instead get a pension from the personal plan or employer's scheme. What you get depends on the type of scheme you contract out through:

- with an employer's final pay pension scheme (see p15), you and your employer pay a lower rate of NI contributions on part of your earnings, and the employer's scheme guarantees you a minimum pension broadly equivalent to SERPS pension. At retirement, the amount of guaranteed pension paid by the employer's scheme is deducted from the SERPS pension. The state pays you whatever amount of SERPS pension remains. So you can never lose by contracting out this way – and you'll probably gain as most employers' schemes expect to pay you more than just the guaranteed amount

- with an employer's money purchase pension scheme (see p15), you and your employer pay a lower rate of NI contributions on part of your earnings, but your employer must pay the amount of contributions saved to buy you certain pension rights (protected rights – see p38). At retirement, your SERPS pension is reduced as if you had been contracted out through a final pay scheme (see opposite). But the protected rights pension that you get from the employer's scheme might be more or less than the amount deducted

- with a personal pension plan, you and your employer pay the full rate of NI contributions as if you were contracted in to SERPS, but the difference between this and the contracted out rate is paid into your personal pension by the Government (it's called the NI rebate). The rebate is used to buy you certain pension rights (protected rights – see p38). At retirement, your SERPS pension is reduced as if you had been contracted out through an employer's final pay scheme (see opposite). But the protected rights pension you get from the personal plan may be more or less than the amount deducted.

All employees now have the freedom to contract out of SERPS, but is it wise to leave the security of the SERPS scheme? Even with the reduction in SERPS benefits coming in from 1998, SERPS maintains a link between your pension and changes in national average earnings before retirement and your SERPS pension increases in line with inflation after retirement. Only by contracting out through an employer's final pay pension scheme can you guarantee to do at least as well as the SERPS pension you give up.

There is no such guarantee with any other type of pension arrangement (ie a personal pension plan or employer's money purchase pension scheme) where the pension you get depends on how well your contributions are invested and how much pension you can buy at retirement.

In practice, younger people may do better contracting out because the longer the NI rebate has to grow, the more likely it is to build up a better pension than the SERPS pension given up. Men will do better than women of the same age, because they retire later – the money has longer to grow. To make contracting out more attractive, the Government is offering a special incentive payment to people newly contracting out of SERPS. This incentive is added to their NI rebate and thus invested in the contracted out scheme or plan, increasing the chance of you gaining rather than losing out. The Table below gives you a very rough indication of whether contracting out is likely to be worthwhile for you.

SHOULD YOU CONSIDER CONTRACTING OUT?

	If you qualify for the incentive	If you don't qualify for the incentive
If you are a woman aged:		
under 25	YES	YES
25 to 35	YES	MAYBE
35 to 40	MAYBE	NO
over 40	NO	NO
If you are a man aged:		
under 35	YES	YES
35 to 45	YES	MAYBE
45 to 50	MAYBE	NO
over 50	NO	NO

The special incentive is payable only up to 5 April 1993, and after that date the amount of rebate paid by the Government is expected to be reduced – these changes will both affect the decision to contract out or not. Also as you become older, there will inevitably come a time when it makes more sense for you to be contracted into SERPS. So you should review your decision every year or two.

GRADUATED PENSION

This is an old state earnings-related pension scheme which ran from 6 April 1961 to 5 April 1975 for people earning over £9 a week at that time. If you belonged to it, every £9 a woman contributed and every £7.50 a man contributed counts as one 'unit'. In the 1989-90 year, you get 5.71p graduated pension a week for each unit you hold. The maximum graduated pension a man can get is presently £4.92 a week, and for a woman £4.11.

Graduated pension increases in line with inflation each year, but will always be relatively small because the graduated scheme was not designed to protect contributors against the high rates of inflation experienced during the early 1970s. Your widow can inherit half your graduated pension; your widower can inherit half your graduated pension but only if he is over 65 and you are over 60 at the time of your death.

You might have been contracted out of the graduated pension scheme. This means that your employer at that time took over responsibility for paying you a pension at retirement (called the Equivalent Pension Benefit, or EPB) instead of the graduated pension you would otherwise have been building up.

ACTION NOW

Step 1: Go back to the route maps in Section 1 to check what action, if any, you should take to protect or boost your state pensions.

Step 2: Check on your state pension entitlement from time to time. The Department of Social Security (DSS) runs a Retirement Pension Forecast and Advice (RPFA) service. You can use this to find out what your pension entitlement is so far, what it's likely to be at retirement, and anything you can do now to increase your entitlement – for example, whether you should make Class 3 contributions, whether it's worth switching to the full rate of Class 1 contributions if you are paying at the married women's reduced rate, and so on. The service can give you forecasts of basic, SERPS and graduated pension. To use the service, you fill in Form BR19 and send it to RPFA Unit, Room 37D, Central Office, Newcastle upon Tyne, NE98 1YX. There is a copy of the form in the back of this Pack and you can get extra copies from any DSS office.

Step 3: Take any steps needed to maximise your state pensions which are suggested by the RPFA service. Then read the other Sections in this Pack which apply to you to find out what other income you might expect in retirement from employers' pension schemes or personal pension plans and consider what extra savings you need to make for retirement.

MORE INFORMATION ABOUT STATE PENSIONS

You may find the following leaflets, available free from DSS offices, useful:

NP27 Looking after someone at home? How to protect your pension

NP38 Your future pension

NP45 Guide to widow's benefits

NP46 A guide to state retirement pensions

SA29 Your social security and pension rights in the European Community

NI1 National Insurance for married women

NI27A National Insurance for people with small earnings from self-employment

NI40 National Insurance for employees

NI41 National Insurance guide for the self-employed

NI42 National Insurance voluntary contributions

NI48 National Insurance – unpaid and late contributions

NI51 National Insurance for widows

NI125 Training for further employment and your National Insurance record

You can find the address of your local DSS office in the phone book under its old title of 'Social Security, Department of Health and' or 'Health and Social Security, Department of'. New phone books should list it as 'Social Security, Department of'.

2

EMPLOYERS' PENSION SCHEMES

Around half of all employees work for an employer who provides a pension scheme. But since 6 April 1988, everyone has the right to leave their employer's scheme, or not to join in the first place.

You'd be very unwise just to opt out of your employer's scheme without making alternative pension arrangements – such as taking out a personal plan (see p24). For many, joining or staying in their employer's scheme will be the best option.

WHAT EMPLOYERS' SCHEMES OFFER

Typically, employers' schemes provide:

- a pension once you retire
- a pension for your widow or widower and possibly other dependants if you die before or after retirement
- help if you have to stop work early through ill-health (and sometimes, if you retire early for other reasons)
- lump sum life insurance to cover you while you are working for the employer – either through the pension scheme or through a separate policy.

At least part of the pensions from contracted out schemes (see p18) must be increased each year, once they are being paid. Most schemes will usually increase the remaining part though these increases might not be guaranteed, or any guarantee might be pitched at a fairly low level such as 3 per cent a year. But many public sector schemes (covering, for example, teachers and local government employees) guarantee to match inflation. And, in practice, quite a lot of private sector schemes pay increases well above their guaranteed level.

Most employers' schemes enjoy considerable tax benefits (see p16), but to qualify they must stick to rules set by the Inland Revenue. If 1989 Budget proposals become law, there will be new-style rules which will apply to new schemes set up from 14 March 1989 and to new members joining existing schemes on or after 1 June 1989. Most existing members of existing schemes will continue to be covered by the old-style rules unless they change scheme. The old- and new-style rules for pensions are:

- under old-style rules, normal retirement dates must lie between the ages of 60 and 75 though earlier retirement is allowed subject to certain conditions. Under new-style rules, retirement must usually be between ages 50 and 70 (but can be as late as 75); you can get the maximum pension as long as you've been with the employer for at least 20 years and your scheme rules allow it. Under both sets of rules, there are earlier retirement ages for some types of employment. In practice, many schemes have a normal retirement date of 65 for men and 60 for women
- under old-style rules, retirement pension can't be more than two-thirds of your 'final pay' (see opposite). Under new-style rules, only pay up to £60,000 will count towards pension (and lump sum – see below), so the maximum pension will be £40,000. The £60,000 limit will be increased each year in line with price inflation
- you can swap part of your pension for a tax-free lump sum but this mustn't be more than one and a half times your final pay. Under old-style rules, there's no limit on the lump sum unless the scheme was set up (or altered) after 17 March 1987, in which case there's a maximum of £150,000. Under new-style rules, the maximum is £90,000 (one and a half times £60,000 – see above)

- under both sets of rules, there can be a widow's, widower's and other dependants' pensions – none of which can be more than two-thirds of the maximum retirement pension you could have got

- pensions being paid can't be increased by more than the amount which would have been needed to inflation-proof the maximum pension you could have got.

These limits apply to the total of your pensions from all employers' pension schemes – not to each scheme individually.

TYPES OF EMPLOYERS' SCHEMES

Final pay schemes

The majority of people in employers' schemes belong to final pay schemes. With these your retirement pension will be based on your pay in the last year or last few years before retirement and on the number of years that you have been a member of the scheme. Commonly, you'll get either one-eightieth or one-sixtieth of your 'final pay' for each year.

'Final pay' can be defined in the scheme rules in a number of ways – for example, pay at a specified date, average earnings over the last three years before retirement,

EXAMPLE

In 1988, Bill retired after 18 years in his employer's pension scheme. His final pay was defined as the average of his best three years' earnings out of the last ten less the amount of the basic state pension (£2,032 per annum at that time). This worked out at £15,682 - £2,132 = £13,550. He got one-sixtieth of this for each year in the scheme, so his pension was 1/60 x 18 x £13,550 = £4,065 a year. The scheme also provided a widow's pension of half Bill's pension. Pensions from the scheme have generally been increased in line with inflation each year, though only increases of 3 per cent a year are guaranteed under the rules.

your best year's earnings out of the last ten years before retirement and so on. It can be restricted to just basic salary, or extended to include overtime, bonuses and commission. If the scheme is specifically designed to provide retirement income on top of the state basic pension, final pay might exclude a slice roughly equal to the single person's basic pension. Check the definition used by your scheme.

Money purchase schemes

This is the other common type of employer's pension scheme. Unlike a final pay scheme, it does not guarantee a pension related to your pay.

Contributions paid by you and your employer are invested. Your pension at retirement depends on how well the investment has grown and on how much pension the investment will buy. The rate at which the investment can be converted into pension is called the 'annuity rate'. Annuity rates vary and how much pension you get may depends critically on the date you take your pension.

3

EXAMPLE

Joe is about to retire after 10 years in a money purchase scheme. During that time he has paid 5 per cent of his pay into the scheme and his employer has paid a further 10 per cent of the amount of Joe's pay. The contributions have grown to a fund of £30,750. At an annuity rate of 10 per cent, the fund is enough to buy him a pension for life of £3,075 increasing by 5 per cent a year. The scheme also provides a widow's pension.

Hybrid schemes

Some schemes include both a final pay element and a money purchase element. For example, a scheme could be basically a money purchase scheme but also guarantee that the pension at retirement would not be less than a certain proportion of your final pay depending on how many years you'd been a member. The scheme would pay you the higher of the final pay element or the money purchase element.

WHAT EMPLOYERS' SCHEMES COST

Some employers' schemes are 'non-contributory' which means that you pay nothing towards the scheme, your employer foots the whole bill. More often, you'll pay a fixed contribution of, say, around 5 per cent of your gross salary into the scheme, and your employer will contribute too. In a final pay scheme, the employer usually undertakes to meet the balance of the cost. In a money purchase scheme, the employer will pay a set amount – usually expressed as a percentage of your pay.

Provided that they are approved by the Inland Revenue (see p14), employers' pension schemes get very favourable treatment from the taxman. Your income tax bill is worked out on your pay after your pension contributions have been deducted – so you get tax relief on your contributions at your highest rate(s) of tax. Your employer also gets tax relief on the contributions he makes. Income and capital gains made by investing the contributions build up tax-free. And you can usually take part of your benefits as a tax-free lump sum at retirement. Your retirement pension counts as taxable income.

The tax breaks are so good that the taxman limits the amount of money you can invest in this way: the most you can pay into an employer's scheme in any one year is 15 per cent of your earnings (including the value of fringe benefits other than various share option schemes). This limit covers your regular contributions as well as any additional contributions (see opposite) you might be making. If 1989 Finance Bill proposals become law, only earnings up to £60,000 will count (this limit will be increased each year in line with price inflation). This will apply to all schemes irrespective of when set up or when you join them. There is no limit on your employer's contributions, so long as the benefits do not exceed the maxima laid down by the Inland Revenue.

LEAVING YOUR SCHEME BEFORE RETIREMENT

If you leave an employer's pension scheme before retirement, what happens to the pension rights you have built up depends on the type of scheme.

Final pay schemes

With a final pay scheme, you are entitled to a 'deferred pension' after two years' membership. This is a pension which will be paid once you reach retirement date and generally it's based on the number of years you belonged to the scheme and on your final pay at the time you left the scheme.

Until quite recently, there was no obligation to increase a deferred pension to cope with inflation – and since it could be as much as forty years between leaving a scheme and reaching retirement age, a deferred pension could be virtually worthless. But for people leaving schemes since 1 January 1986, any deferred pension you've built up since 1 January 1985 will have to be increased by inflation between the time you leave the scheme and the date you reach retirement or at a rate of 5 per cent a year if this is lower. Note that if the scheme is contracted out of SERPS (see p18), the part that you get instead of SERPS pension (the GMP) must be increased at a higher rate.

Even with this protection, a deferred pension is likely to be a lot less than the pension you'd have got if you'd stayed in the scheme until retirement. This is because it's based on fewer years and on your pay on leaving the job, not your pay at retirement.

Money purchase schemes

If you leave a money purchase scheme after two years' membership, you cease contributing to the scheme, and your employer stops making contributions on your behalf. But the contributions already made continue to be invested and you get the benefit of the total sum built up by retirement.

Transferring your pension rights

Instead of leaving the pension from a job you've left to be paid out by the original employer's scheme at retirement, you can transfer your pension rights to another employer's scheme, a personal pension plan or a special personal plan called a Section 32 plan. You might want to transfer your pension rights in this way if you think you can get a better pension or other benefits than you'll get by leaving it in the old employer's scheme.

The value of your pension rights is known as the transfer value. In a final pay scheme, the transfer value is a lump sum which is judged (by an actuary) to be enough if invested now to provide the deferred pension at retirement. In a money purchase scheme, it's the value of the fund built up by the invested contributions at the transfer date.

Less than two years' membership?

If you leave an employer's pension scheme before two years' membership are up, you'll probably just be offered a refund of your own contributions. Interest will often be added, but tax deducted at a special rate of 20 per cent. If the employer's scheme is contracted out of SERPS, there may be a further deduction to buy you back into SERPS.

You do not get the benefit of, or refund of, any contributions made by your employer on your behalf. If you leave a scheme after two years, you are not allowed to have a refund (except for any contributions you paid before April 1975). In practice, some schemes will let you have a deferred pension even if you have been a member for less than two years.

BOOSTING YOUR PENSION

If you want to increase the pension, or other benefits, that you'll get from an employer's pension scheme, you can do this by making Additional Voluntary Contributions (AVCs). All employers' schemes must accept AVCs. Alternatively, you can pay your AVCs into a special personal plan called a Free Standing Additional Voluntary Contribution (FSAVC) scheme, which you take out independently of your employer's scheme.

FSAVC schemes and many AVC schemes work on the money purchase principle. Your contributions are invested and build up a fund which you can use at retirement to buy extra benefits in your employer's scheme, for example, extra pension, extra widow's pension, or increases to your pension once it's being paid. Some AVC schemes buy added years in the employer's main scheme which increase your entitlement to pension and other benefits.

You can't use an AVC or FSAVC scheme to provide, or increase, the tax-free lump sum you take on retirement, unless you joined the scheme or took it out before 8 April 1987. And you can't use AVCs or FSAVCs to increase benefits beyond the Inland Revenue limits (see p14). In the past, you couldn't get back any 'excess' AVCs if you over-contributed, so they could be wasted. But, if 1989 Budget proposals become law, at retirement, you'll get back any excess AVCs after a tax deduction, broadly in line with the tax benefits given. This will apply to people retiring on or after the day the proposals become law (probably late July).

3

AVCs and FSAVCs count as part of the 15 per cent limit on contributions along with your ordinary contributions (if any) to the main employer's scheme.

The running costs of an employer's AVC scheme are often lower than with an FSAVC scheme. If this is so, the employer's AVC scheme allows more of your contributions to be invested for your benefit. You might also find that AVCs can be used to provide a wider range of benefits than FSAVCs.

On the other hand, your employer's AVC scheme might not give you the investment choice that you want. FSAVCs allow you to invest your money in different ways – for example, through a unit-linked or with-profits plan. The range of FSAVCs is similar to the types of personal pension plans on offer – see p27 for details.

CONTRACTING OUT

You can be contracted out of the State Earnings Related Pension Scheme (SERPS) through membership of an employer's pension scheme. You pay lower NI contributions on part of your pay and give up part of your SERPS pension at retirement. Instead, you get a pension from the employer's scheme. How much you get depends on the type of scheme.

Final pay schemes
Most final pay schemes are 'contracted out' of SERPS. At state pension age, you'll get a pension from your employer's scheme which is broadly equivalent to the SERPS pension given up (known as the Guaranteed Minimum Pension – GMP). If your pension worked out according to the scheme's normal formula comes to less than your GMP, the scheme must increase your pension to the amount of the GMP. The amount of GMP is deducted from your SERPS pension at retirement and the state pays whatever SERPS pension remains. The calculation is repeated each year to take account of increases in SERPS pension and the GMP. You can't lose pension by contracting out through a final pay scheme.

From April 1990, the employer's scheme will increase the GMP by 3 per cent a year, or the rate of inflation if this is less, for pension earned from 6 April 1988 onwards.

Money purchase schemes
Money purchase schemes can also contract out of SERPS, but the pension from the scheme won't normally equal the SERPS pension given up – it could be more or less. Your employer must contribute a minimum percentage of your earnings into a pension scheme which buys what are known as 'protected rights': a pension for you and a widow's or widower's pension. The amount of pension you get under these protected rights – like any other money purchase scheme – depends on how well the invested contributions grow and the annuity rate at the time of taking the pension. At retirement, your SERPS pension is reduced by a notional amount equal to the GMP you would have got if you had been contracted out through a final pay scheme rather than a money purchase scheme. The state pays whatever SERPS pension remains. This calculation is repeated each year to take account of increases in SERPS and the 'notional' GMP. The pension you get from the contracted out money purchase scheme could be more or less than the SERPS pension you give up. Once the protected rights pension is being paid, it must be increased by 3 per cent a year, or the rate of inflation if lower.

The amount your employer must contribute on your behalf is the difference between the Class 1 NI contributions payable on your earnings if contracted in to SERPS and the amount payable when contracted out. For the 1989-90 contribution year, this is 5.8 per cent of your earnings between the Lower and Upper Earnings Limits. Of this, 3.8 per cent represents the saving on your employer's NI contributions and 2 per cent the saving on your NI contributions.

Your employer may require you to contribute your part of the savings, and deduct it from your pay. If so, it will qualify for tax relief at your top rate(s) of tax in the same way as any other pension contribution. But you get this tax relief directly – it is not paid into the pension scheme.

Contracting out through your own plan

If your employer's scheme is not contracted out of SERPS, you can contract out by yourself and still remain in your employer's scheme. You can do this either through an FSAVC scheme – see p17 – or a Minimum Appropriate Personal Pension (MAPP) – see p27.

With both, you continue to pay Class 1 NI contributions as if you were in SERPS (ie at the full rate). But the extra over the contracted out rates is paid into the plan or scheme by the DSS to provide protected rights. If you want to contract out on your own, you'd do better to take out a MAPP. With this, you'll get basic rate tax relief on part of the rebate paid into the plan; with an FSAVC scheme, you won't.

Incentive payments

If your job (rather than you) has not been contracted out through your present scheme, or through another scheme with the same employer, since 1 January 1986, you will also be entitled to a Government incentive of 2 per cent of your earnings between the Lower and Upper Earnings Limits for each year up to 5 April 1993. This must be paid into the scheme and used to provide protected rights, if the scheme is a contracted out money purchase scheme. You'll also be entitled to the incentive if you are newly contracted out through a final pay scheme.

PROS AND CONS OF EMPLOYERS' PENSION SCHEMES

The following points will help you to decide whether your employer's scheme is suitable for you, or whether you should be considering a personal pension plan instead. The first few apply to all employers' pension schemes; those that follow depend on whether your emploeer offers a final pay scheme or a money purchase scheme.

All employers' schemes

pro

In most schemes, your employer pays in more than you do (in non-contributory schemes he bears the whole cost). Your employer is unlikely to contribute to any personal pension arrangements you make if he runs his own scheme, and by yourself you might not be able to afford benefits comparable to those in your employer's scheme

pro

An employer's scheme – particularly a final pay scheme – may start to look more and more attractive as you get older because the cost of providing for your pension rises. But if you've chosen to opt out of your employer's scheme, you might not be allowed to change your mind later. So find out whether you can join or rejoin later before taking any decisions

pro

The administration costs of running an employer's scheme generally work out a lot lower per person than the costs of running a personal pension plan, and the employer often bears all the administration costs of his scheme. So in an employer's scheme more of the contributions are left to invest for benefits

pro/con

Your employer's scheme probably covers a whole package of benefits including widow's pension, possibly children's pensions, benefits for early retirement through ill-health, and so on. If you take out a personal pension plan, you'll need to make sure that you make adequate provision for dependants as well as for your own pension. On the other hand, you may not want all the benefits offered by an employer's scheme, and a personal pension plan might let you tailor benefits more closely to your needs: But be careful to alter your benefits as your circumstances change – for example, if you marry or have children

Final pay schemes

pro

If you are a member of the same final pay scheme for many years up to retirement, you have the security of knowing that your pension is growing as your earnings grow because of the link to final pay. This may be particularly useful if you expect to make a career within one company

pro

If you belong to a final pay scheme, you know that your pension will be a proportion of your final pay (whatever your pre-retirement final pay turns out to be). This will help you to decide whether your retirement income is likely to be adequate (as a percentage of your pay at retirement) or whether you should be making extra pension savings now

con

If you change jobs soon after joining a final pay scheme, the benefits you get might not add up to much. If you expect to change jobs several times, final pay schemes may not be best for you. This may well be the case if, for example, you are young, or you are a woman who expects to take career breaks to raise a family

con

In final pay schemes, younger people get less benefit from the contributions paid in than older members nearing retirement, so if you are in your 20s, or 30s, say, you might do better with a personal pension plan even if your employer doesn't contribute to it

Money purchase schemes

pro

If you leave a money purchase or hybrid scheme early, you can leave your invested contributions to carry on growing. So these schemes may be worth joining even if you do expect to change jobs several times

Step 1: go back to the first route map in Section 1 and check the options you should consider.

Step 2: before you can make any decisions about whether an employer's scheme or a personal pension plan is best for you, you'll need to have information about your employer's scheme. In the back of this Pack, Sheet B *What you should know about your employer's scheme* is a checklist to record details of all the points covered in this Section. Your scheme should have an explanatory booklet which will provide you with many of the answers, and the trustees' annual report will give you some more; for other information or explanation of anything that you don't understand, you should talk to the officials of your scheme – the trustees, the pensions manager or pensions administrator. Your personnel department should be able to tell you who to contact and how, if it is not clear from the scheme literature.

Step 3: if you already belong to your employer's scheme, get a recent 'benefit statement'. This should show what you can expect if you stay until retirement, and what you'll get if you leave now. The statement should help you decide whether your retirement income is likely to be adequate, or whether you should be considering extra pension savings now. And most financial advisers (see p29) should compare the likely benefits from your employer's scheme with the benefits being offered by any personal pension plan. If you don't already have a recent statement, ask the scheme officials to provide one.

Step 4: it's quite likely that by the time you reach retirement, you may have been a member of a number of different employers' schemes and may be expecting bits of pension from several sources. It's easy to lose touch with old schemes, especially if the company changes hands, or you move house. In the back of this Pack, you'll find Sheet C *Keeping track of your employers' pensions*, which is a handy place to keep a note of old schemes. Your record sheet might look something like the example overleaf:

3

KEEPING TRACK OF YOUR EMPLOYERS' PENSIONS

Name and address of company, or scheme administrator	Date last checked	Membership number	Date joined scheme	Date left scheme	Action on leaving [1]	Last address you gave the scheme
Workin Ltd. 31 Payday Road Wembley Middlesex	12·5·66	W1543	21·7·61	1·5·66	Refund bought back into state graduated scheme	n.a.
~~Keepbusy Ltd.~~ ~~Union Estate~~ ~~Stevenage~~	~~10·6·73~~	~~678-AA~~	~~1·6·66~~	~~12·12·72~~	~~Deferred pension~~	26 Ogilvy St. Wembley Middlesex
Baby Industries (took over Keepbusy) Union Estate Stevenage	24·5·78	678-MKB	1·6·66	12·12·72	Deferred pension	26 Ogilvy St. Wembley Middlesex

Notes
[1] Give details of whether benefits transferred, to be paid from old scheme or contributions repaid to you. Note also whether any EPB, and/or GMP is payable from scheme at state pension age.

The record sheet tells you:

Name and address of company or scheme administrator and date last checked: check and update this, if necessary, whenever the company communicates with you. Make sure you note the date so that you have some check on whether you have a recent address

Membership number: number you should quote in any contact with the scheme so that your records can be easily traced

Date joined scheme and **Date left scheme:** useful information if you need to correspond with the scheme about your benefits

Action on leaving: make a note here of whether you have a deferred pension with the scheme, whether the scheme will be paying you any GMP or protected rights, whether you were bought back into SERPS, whether you transferred your pension rights elsewhere, and whether you took a refund of contributions. This will give you a check on whether you are due to be paid anything by the scheme when you reach retirement

Last address you gave scheme: you don't need to fill this in if you are sure that you are not due any benefits from the old scheme. But if you are, note the address that the scheme has for you, and make sure you write to it giving the scheme your new address every time you move.

When an entry becomes out of date, cross it out and replace with the updated information. If you can't find the relevant documents about a pension and you are out of touch with the scheme, make enquiries now – don't wait until retirement.

Your major source of information about your employer's scheme is the scheme officials themselves – the trustees, the pensions manager or administrator – and possibly your personnel department at work.

For more general information about employers' schemes, such as the laws applying to them and common practice, you could contact:

Company Pensions Information Centre (CPIC), 7 Old Park Lane, London W1Y 3LJ (telephone: 01-493 4757).

CPIC also publish a number of useful booklets explaining how pension schemes work.

If you have problems with your employer's scheme – for example, you can't get the information or help that you need, or you are in dispute over the benefits you expect – you could seek advice from:

Occupational Pensions Advisory Service, 8a Bloomsbury Square, London WC1A 2UA (telephone queries handled weekdays 11am to 3pm on 01-831 5511).

The Service can't arbitrate between you and the scheme but it can advise on your position and may be able to present your case to the scheme for you.

For a fee, you can get independent advice and help in comparing your employer's pension with other options, by contacting a member of either:

Society of Pension Consultants, Ludgate House, Ludgate Circus, London EC4A 2AB,

or

Association of Consulting Actuaries, Rolls House, 7 Rolls Lane, Fetter Lane, London EC4A 1NH.

Both organisations can provide you with a list of members.

3

PERSONAL PENSION PLANS

With personal pension plans, you make your own pension arrangements directly with an insurance company, friendly society, unit trust, bank or building society (the plan provider), rather than through a scheme organised by an employer or the state.

Since 1956, the self-employed and employees not in an employer's scheme have been able to contribute to personal plans (called Section 226 plans). Since 1 July 1988, these plans have been superceded by new-style personal pension plans. These new plans can be used to contract out of the State Earnings Related Pension Scheme (SERPS) if you are an employee. But even if you wish to remain in SERPS, a personal pension plan may be an ideal way of topping up your SERPS pension.

HOW PERSONAL PENSION PLANS WORK

Personal pension plans are all money purchase schemes: you make contributions which are invested in the plan (a generous employer might also contribute). When you draw the pension, the fund built up in your plan is used to buy an annuity from an insurance company or friendly society: this provides an income for life. The amount of pension you get depends on how well the invested contributions grow, and on the rate ('annuity rate') at which you can convert the proceeds of your plan into pension. You can use the proceeds to provide benefits other than just retirement pension. For example, you can include a widow's, or widower's, pension.

You can also draw some of the proceeds as a tax-free lump sum – see page 31. Using the proceeds for a lump sum or for other benefits will reduce the amount left to be used for retirement pension.

You can also use part of your contributions to provide benefits during your working life – for example, life insurance, or a pension for a widow, widower or children, if you should die before retirement, or a pension to be paid out if you have to give up work early through ill health.

EXAMPLE

Judith, who is 35, pays £30 a month into a personal pension plan. Her plan is estimated to be worth £75,000 by the time she reaches age 60, assuming her investment grows at a rate of 8.5 per cent a year. If annuity rates at the time she reaches 60 are, say, 8 per cent, her plan would provide a pension of £6,000. (If inflation averaged 7 per cent a year over the next 25 years, the pension would be worth £1,100 a year in terms of today's money.) Alternatively, she could take up to £18,750 as a tax-free lump sum (worth £3,454 in today's money) which would leave her with a pension of £4,500 (worth £830 at today's prices).

To a large extent, you can choose a package of benefits to suit your particular circumstances. Personal pension plans enjoy considerable tax benefits (see opposite), so there are some restrictions set by the Inland Revenue on retirement age, and the amount contributed.

Retirement age

You can normally take the proceeds of a personal pension plan at any age from 50 to 75. The exception to this is with a personal pension plan which is used to contract out of SERPS: the protected rights pension from this can't be taken until you reach state pension age.

Some plans may require you to set a retirement date at the time you take out the plan – though there's usually no penalty for retiring later. But there may be penalties for retiring before the retirement date you choose at the start, so it's probably best to choose the earliest likely date. Though retiring at 50 may seem an attractive option, in practice it's unlikely to be financially feasible. The earlier you retire, the less pension you'll get, because your pension has had less time to build up, yet it has to be paid out for longer. But you do not need actually to retire at the plan retirement date: you can draw the pension but carry on working. By using several personal pension plans (you can have more than one at a time), you could wind down your working life, gradually replacing earned income with pension as you reduce the hours you work.

The amount of pension

When you begin to draw the pension, the fund built up by your invested contributions is used to buy an annuity which provides an income for life. The amount of income you get from this lump sum depends on the annuity rate and this depends on the level of interest rates in the economy at the time – the higher annuity rates are, the more pension you'll get. With some personal pension plans, you may be guaranteed a certain annuity rate (so you can be sure of the amount of pension you'll get for a given lump sum); but you might do better if annuity rates are higher than this guaranteed rate.

If your pension stays the same each year, its buying power could be quickly eaten away by inflation. You can choose a pension which increases each year (by 3 per cent or 5 per cent, for example), but it will be smaller to start with. For example, a pension which increases by 5 per cent compound a year will start off at around three-quarters of the amount of a level pension and overtake the level pension only after six years. Some pension providers offer an index-linked pension (one which rises in line with inflation as measured by the Retail Prices Index), but this will usually start off much lower than the level pension.

Switching plans

You don't have to stay with the same personal pension plan until retirement. You can stop contributing but leave your money invested, in which case, the plan becomes 'paid up'. Or, you can transfer the fund which has built up to another plan, or to an employer's scheme if it agrees to accept the transfer. But there may be penalties for stopping a plan early. And there may be a loyalty bonus if you stay with a plan for a specified length of time or a retirement bonus if you stay with it until retirement.

At retirement, you can take the fund that has built up and use it to buy a pension from another provider – this is called exercising the 'open market option'. But occasionally there's a bonus if you stay with the original plan provider.

WHAT PERSONAL PENSION PLANS COST

With some plans, you agree to make contributions regularly – each month or year, say. With others, you contribute a single lump sum payment (called a 'single premium'). The plan providers may set minimum contributions that they'll accept, for example £10 or £20 a month, £200 a year, or £500 for a single premium plan. Most regular contribution plans will allow you to increase your contributions regularly, and make extra one-off contributions.

Provided they are approved by the Inland Revenue, personal pension plans get very favourable tax treatment. Contributions to a personal pension scheme qualify for tax relief (if your employer contributes, he also gets tax relief on the contributions). Income and capital gains made by investing the contributions build up tax-free. You can take part of your benefits as a tax-free lump sum at retirement (though not any part of

4

protected rights – see p27). And your retirement pension counts as taxable income.

If you are an employee, you hand over to the plan provider contributions with basic rate tax deducted; the plan provider claims the tax back from the Inland Revenue and adds it to your plan. If you are a higher rate taxpayer, you'll need to claim the extra tax relief. If you are self-employed, you pay your contributions gross (ie before deducting any tax), and claim the full amount of the tax relief from the taxman.

EXAMPLE

Albert, who's employed by an engineering firm, wants to contribute £100 a month to his personal pension plan. He pays £75 a month into the plan. The plan provider claims basic rate tax of £25 (at the 1989-90 tax rate) and adds it to the plan, making a contribution of £100 in total.

There are limits on the amount you can invest in personal pension plans which will qualify for tax relief. If 1989 Budget proposals become law, in any year up to age 35, you can't invest more than 17.5 per cent of your net relevant earnings (basically your earnings for tax purposes). As you get older, you'll be able to invest more. But you can't get tax relief on any contributions relating to earnings over £60,000 a year.

These new limits apply from the 1989-90 tax year onwards. The percentage limits for earlier years, and for Section 226 plans are lower (see Table) but there is no £60,000 ceiling on the earnings they relate to. If you have a Section 226 plan *and* a new personal pension plan, you can invest up to the lower percentage limit in your Section 226 plan, and if you're still below the maximum limit for personal plans, you can invest in that plan too.

MAXIMUM YOU CAN INVEST IN A PERSONAL PENSION PLAN OR SECTION 226 PLAN

Age on 6 April of tax year	Maximum you can contribute (as percentage of earnings)	
	to personal pension plan from 1989-90	to Section 226 plan
Up to 35	17.5	17.5
36 to 45	20	17.5
46 to 50	25	17.5
51 to 55	30	20
56 to 60	35	22.5
61 and over	35	27.5

You can get tax relief on contributions above these limits if you have unused relief from the previous six years – you use up the unused relief from the earliest year first. But, if you are an employee, you do not count as having unused relief for any period in which you were a member of an employer's scheme. You can also ask for a contribution paid in the current tax year to be carried back and treated as if it had been paid in the last tax year.

If you are employed, your employer can contribute to your personal pension plan (though those running their own schemes probably won't). Your employer's contributions count towards the limit on contributions. They can't be carried back to the previous tax year.

You can contribute up to 5 per cent of your earnings to pay for life insurance: whatever you contribute towards this counts towards your overall limit for personal pension contributions. (You can, of course, take out life insurance separately but you won't then get tax relief on the payments you make.)

CONTRACTING OUT

You can use a personal pension plan to 'contract out' of the State Earnings Related Pension Scheme (SERPS) – see p9. You give up part of your SERPS pension and instead get a pension from your personal pension plan. The pension may be more or less than the SERPS pension you give up. This option is not available to the self-employed as they don't belong to SERPS.

If you use a personal pension plan to contract out of SERPS, you go on paying the higher contracted in rate of Class 1 NI contributions. But the DSS pays the difference between the higher rate and lower rate of NI contributions into your personal pension plan – this is known as the NI rebate. The DSS will pay the rebate only into a personal pension plan which provides what are known as protected rights benefits, which are a pension at state retirement age and a widow's or widower's pension.

For the tax years from 6 April 1988 to 5 April 1993, the amount of the NI rebate is 5.8 per cent of earnings between the Lower and Upper Earnings Limits. Two per cent is a rebate of your contributions and 3.8 per cent is a rebate of your employer's contributions. The rebate of your contributions qualifies for basic rate (but not higher rate) tax relief, so the DSS adds approximately another 0.67 per cent in the 1988-89 tax year in respect of basic rate tax at 25 per cent, making a total rebate of roughly 6.47 per cent of earnings between the Lower and Upper Earnings Limits.

The Government will pay a special incentive to people newly contracting out of SERPS through a personal pension plan. The incentive is 2 per cent of earnings between the Lower and Upper Earnings Limits, and it is payable up to the end of the 1992-93 tax year. You'll count as newly contracted out unless you have voluntarily left your present employer's contracted out scheme since 5 April 1988 having been a member for at least two years. In the back of this Pack, Sheet D *What the Government contributes to your contracted out personal pension plan,* shows the amount of rebate, and incentive if applicable, that you qualify for depending on your earnings.

If you are in an employer's pension scheme which doesn't contract out of SERPS, you can contract out yourself by taking out a special personal pension plan called a Minimum Appropriate Personal Pension (MAPP). With MAPPs, the rebates and incentives are the only contributions which can be invested in the plan. Note that the DSS rebates and incentives do not count towards the yearly contribution limits for personal pension plans.

HOW YOUR MONEY IS INVESTED

There are different ways of investing the money in your personal pension plan which give you different balances of risk and expected return. There's no way of predicting future investment returns, but the general rule is: the more risk you take, the greater your chance of a higher return.

Under current rules, you can choose the type of plan you want and broadly how the plan provider invests your money. But, if 1989 Budget proposals become law, you'll also be able to choose a plan where you pick your own investments as long as you stick to certain types (including UK and overseas shares, unit trusts, British Government stocks, insurance company managed funds, and deposit accounts).

Deposit-based schemes and deposit administration plans

Deposit-based schemes are offered by some building societies, and could also be offered by banks. Deposit administration plans are much the same but are offered by life insurance companies.

Your money is invested in an account to which interest is added at intervals (the rate isn't guaranteed). The amount of your capital grows as interest is added and can never fall, making these schemes low risk. But they are vulnerable to inflation – the value of your plan is unlikely to keep pace if inflation is high.

4

These plans can be useful if you are getting close to retirement – within a year or two, say. But they are not suitable if you have longer to leave your money invested.

With-profits plans

These are offered by life insurance companies or friendly societies. Your money is invested by the company in a broad spread of investments – shares, Government stocks, property, and so on. The return that you get depends on how well the company's investments do, and on factors such as the expenses the company faces and its policy on distributing profits from its business.

Your return comes in the form of bonuses: 'reversionary bonuses' are added to your plan at set intervals, for example every year, or every three years. Once added, reversionary bonuses can't be taken away. The level of future bonuses can be changed, but in practice companies tend to keep them fairly stable from year to year. You may also get a 'terminal bonus' when the plan matures at your retirement date. Terminal bonuses can amount to a sizeable proportion of your return – as much as half in some cases – and are not guaranteed. The amount can vary greatly depending, in part, on the value of underlying investments at the time your plan matures.

With-profits plans are a medium risk way of investing. The amount of your capital will rise as bonuses are added and can't fall. You are ultimately investing in a broad range of investments whose capital value can be expected to rise steadily over time, so you should be protected to some extent from inflation as well. The main risk is that the terminal bonus turns out to be lower than you'd hoped.

Unit-linked and unit trust plans

Unit-linked plans are offered by many insurance companies and can be offered by friendly societies; unit trust plans are similar but are offered by some unit trust companies. With a unit-linked plan, your money is allocated to units whose value is linked to a specific fund of investments. With a unit trust plan, your money buys units in a unit trust which is a pool of investments. With both, your return depends on the value of your units; their value rises and falls as the value of the underlying investments in the fund or trust rises and falls.

There are different types of funds and trusts, so you can choose to link your plan to, say, UK shares, foreign shares, government stocks, a managed fund or general trust investing in a broad mixture of investments, and so on. Generally, you can choose to invest in more than one fund or trust – though there may be a minimum investment for each – and you can usually switch between them. The more specialist funds and trusts are the more risky; for most people a managed fund or general trust will be the most appropriate choice because it reduces risk by spreading your money across a good range of different investments.

These plans are higher risk than deposit-type plans or with-profits plans because the amount of your investment can fall – so gains made can subsequently be lost, and your plan could even at times be worth less than the amount of money you've contributed. But over the long term, you'd expect the general trend in the value of your investment to be upwards. In recent decades, these plans would have given you the best chance of keeping ahead of inflation.

Unitised with-profits funds

Some insurance companies have recently started to offer a new type of fund within their unit-linked plans (or, with a few companies, as a seperate plan). You can invest part or all of your money in a unitised with-profits fund, and switch between this and other funds in the normal way. But in the with-profits fund, the amount of your capital can't fall. Your money grows in two ways: the value of the units is regularly increased to reflect the prices of the underlying investments – though the company reserves the right to adjust the way it calculates these values; and at intervals bonus units are added to your holding to reflect the earnings made by the underlying investments (this is similar to the reversionary bonus you would get with a with-profits policy). Once added, the bonus units can't be taken away. These funds give you a medium risk/return option within the generally higher risk unit-linked type of plan.

Which type?

A sensible choice for anyone with many years to go before retirement would be to put some of their money into unit-linked and unit trust plans, and some into with-profits plans. If you are within just a year or two of retirement, you would be wise to watch for a good opportunity (when unit values are high) to switch to a deposit-type investment so that you can ensure that your previous gains won't be lost. Most unit-linked and unit trust plans offer a fund or trust which enables you to switch to a deposit-type method of investment.

BUYING A PERSONAL PENSION PLAN

You can buy personal pension plans direct from plan providers (insurance companies, unit trusts, and so on). Or you can buy through a financial adviser, such as a company representative, independent intermediary, accountant or solicitor.

Under the new Financial Services Act, all financial advisers must either sell the products of just one company, or be completely independent and advise you from the full range of products on the market. Some banks and building societies sell their own personal pension plans, but others act as independent intermediaries. Some financial advisers have 'tied' to a particular plan provider (usually an insurance company) rather than being independent. All accountants and solicitors must give independent advice, if they choose to sell pensions (or other investments).

When you buy a with-profits, unit-linked or unit trust personal pension plan, you are covered by the Financial Services Act, which includes the following:

- people and firms engaged in investment business must be 'authorised'. They must be 'fit and proper' and financially sound. They must conduct their business according to certain rules

- all advisers must find out enough about you to 'know you as a customer'. They must then give you the 'best advice' they can from the range of products they are allowed to sell and the other options open to you, such as being a member of an employer's pension scheme or taking out a deposit-based plan

- advertisements and illustrations that you can be given to demonstrate the possible benefits of a plan must follow rules designed to guard against you being given a misleading impression

- there are compensation schemes to pay at least part of your losses if you lose money through a plan provider or financial adviser going bust and you can't get your money back from them.

Deposit-based plans, such as those offered by some building societies, do not count as investments under the Act and are not covered by it. Though there are regulations (under the Social Security Act 1986) and compensation schemes applying to deposit-based schemes, they fall short of the requirements of the Financial Services Act. In particular, someone selling just deposit-based schemes does not have to get to know you as a customer and does not have to give you best advice.

You should bear in mind that most financial advisers are paid in full, or in part, by getting commission on the plans that they sell you. Ultimately, consumers foot the bill for this commission through the charges or expenses built into the plan (see below). It's a good idea to ask the adviser how much commission he stands to make by selling you a particular plan and to get a second opinion if you think the commission might be unduly influencing the advice given.

4

An independent intermediary must tell you how much commission he'll make on a plan, if you ask. From 1 January 1990, it's proposed that the plan provider must in any case tell you how much commission the independent adviser will make – though not until up to 14 days after you've been sold the plan. Until 1 January, the adviser may or may not volunteer the amount of commission he'll get. If he says the amount will be in line with the 'Maximum Commission Agreement', see Sheet E in the back of this Pack.

Expenses and charges

The rate of interest paid on deposit-based and deposit administration plans is usually partly influenced by the expenses of the plan provider – expenses are not generally made explicit. But with some plans of this type expenses are separated out.

For with-profits plans, the expenses of the company are just one of the factors influencing the level of bonuses and are not separately stated (though proposals are currently being looked at to require insurance companies to disclose some details about expenses).

The situation is quite different for unit-linked and unit trust plans. With these, the companies cover the expenses related to the plans by making various charges direct to the plan holder. Charges are levied in a variety of ways as shown in the Box below.

CHARGES FOR UNIT TRUST AND UNIT-LINKED PLANS

For both unit trust and unit-linked plans:

Bid-offer spread: the difference between the (higher) offer price at which you are allocated or buy units and the (lower) bid price at which you cash in units. Typically this will be around 6 per cent

Management charges: a yearly charge set against the fund or trust to cover the costs of managing the underlying investments – typically around 1 to 1.5 per cent a year

One-off administration charge: there might be a single charge at the outset of the plan, or deducted from the first year's premiums.

In addition, for unit-linked plans:

Policy fee and/or administration charge: a deduction made at regular intervals to cover setting up and paperwork involved in running the plan

Unit allocation: a certain percentage of your contributions is allocated to units – this might be a lower percentage in earlier years, or if you pay monthly rather than yearly, say. Don't be misled by allocations of over 100 per cent – they usually mean 100 per cent of your contribution after a policy or administration fee has been deducted which works out at less than 100 per cent of your total contribution

Capital units: you may be allocated 'special' units especially in the first year or two of the plan. Typically they carry a higher management charge – for example, 3 or 5 per cent a year (compared with, say, 1 to 1.5 per cent for other units) – which you carry on paying throughout the life of the plan, and you might not be credited with their full value if you stop, or transfer, the plan in the early years. Capital units might be converted to ordinary (accumulation) units when the retirement date you originally selected is reached

Surrender charges: you're credited with only a proportion of the value of your plan if you stop, or transfer, it in the early years.

Unit-linked plans may also make a charge if you switch your money from one fund to another – but often the first switch or two each year is free. With unit trust plans, switching from one trust to another could be expensive if you have to sell units in one fund and buy afresh in another, but some plans make use of 'umbrella funds' which enable you to invest in just one trust which is split into several different funds between which you can switch in a similar way to a unit-linked plan.

WHAT IF YOU HAVE A SECTION 226 PLAN?

People who took out personal pensions before 1 July 1988 have what is known as a Section 226 pension plan. These are no longer available but if you already have one you can continue to pay, and increase, contributions to it.

Should you switch instead to a new-style personal pension plan? The main points to consider are:

- you can take out one or more personal pension plans as well as keeping up your Section 226 plan (though running two or more pension plans may cost you more in charges than running just one)

- you don't have to decide now – you can put off switching until you want to start taking a pension

- over the age of 35, you can usually make higher contributions to a personal plan than to a Section 226 plan (if 1989 Budget proposals become law). You can take advantage of these while still keeping up your Section 226 plan as well (see p26)

- with a Section 226 plan, you can start taking your pension at any time between ages 60 and 75. With a personal pension plan, you can start at any time between 50 and 75 (except with protected rights pension – see p24)

- with a Section 226 plan, you can usually get a bigger tax-free lump sum on retirement – up to three times the remaining pension; with a personal pension plan it's a quarter of the value of your fund after subtracting any amount relating to protected rights (assuming 1989 Budget changes become law). If your Section 226 plan was taken out before 17 March 1987, there is no upper limit on the size of lump sum that you can have. For Section 226 plans taken out from that date, the tax-free lump sum can't be more than £150,000 per plan. If 1989 Budget proposals become law, from 6 April 1989, there will be no upper cash limit on the lump sum from a personal pension plan

- you can't use a Section 226 plan to contract out of SERPS. This may be important if you are an employee – see p10 for guidance on who should consider contracting out.

PROS AND CONS OF PERSONAL PENSION PLANS

pro
You can move from job to job, and from being employed to being self-employed and vice versa, without interrupting your pension arrangements – personal pension plans are truly portable plans which go with you not with your job

con
Because benefits from a personal pension plan depend on the amount contributed, how well the contributions grow and annuity rates when you retire, you don't have much idea in advance of how much pension you'll get; this makes planning difficult

con
Benefits aren't automatically linked to earnings as in a final pay employer's

scheme or SERPS to provide some protection against inflation

pro
You can use a personal pension plan to contract out of SERPS. Note that this doesn't mean that you have to leave a contracted-in employer's scheme – you can take out a Minimum Appropriate Personal Pension

con
You might gain or lose pension by contracting out through a personal pension plan – you take the risk

con
Your employer may not be prepared to contribute to your personal pension plan, so you may need to set aside more

4

money yourself to provide benefits comparable to those of an employer's scheme

pro

You can tailor a personal pension plan to your personal needs, whereas with an employer's scheme you contribute towards a package of benefits not all of which may be applicable to you

con

Even if your employer does contribute to your personal pension plan, the maximum amount of contributions that can be made by you and the employer is lower than the maximum contributions to an employers's scheme, though if 1989 Budget proposals to increase

personal pension plan contribution limits become law this is unlikely to be a problem for many people

pro

If benefits from all your employer's schemes and AVCs are close to the Inland Revenue limits, you could switch to a personal pension plan – the benefits from this won't count towards the limits. This is unlikely to be a problem for most people

con

The costs of running personal pension plans are likely to be higher per person than the costs of running an employer's pension scheme, so less of your money is likely to be used for investment with a personal pension plan

ACTION NOW

Step 1: first, decide whether a personal pension plan might be right for you, and whether you should be contracted out of SERPS. Go back to the route maps in Section 1 to check your choices.

Step 2: if a personal pension plan looks like an option you should consider, set about collecting the information you need – details of state pensions, details of your employer's scheme if there is one, details of any pension plans you already have, details of your circumstances, what you can afford to pay, and what you want from a personal pension plan.

Step 3: turn to the back of this Pack and find the *Directory of personal pension plans*. Pick out the plans which have the features that you want. The page references at the top of each column in the Directory refer you back to the relevant sections of this booklet, if you need a detailed explanation of what the columns mean.

Step 4: if your needs are clear-cut and you have a good idea of the plans you are interested in, you can usually contact the plan providers direct (the Directory gives phone numbers) and ask to discuss your

situation with their representative. In many cases, your decision won't be quite so obvious and you'll need detailed advice. Whether you talk to a company representative, or an independent adviser, take along all the information you've collected at Step 2 above. In the back of this Pack, Sheet F *Guide to buying a personal pension plan through a financial adviser* gives you a quick checklist of points to watch out for when using a salesman or intermediary. And Sheet H *What you should know about a personal pension plan* is a checklist to take with you to fill in the details during your meeting with the salesman or intermediary; you'll then have a useful record of the important features of the plan and this can also be compared with the details of other plans.

Step 5: use Sheet 1 *Keeping track of your personal pension plans* in the back of this Pack to keep a handy summary of the plans you have taken out. Your record sheet might look something like the example opposite.

KEEPING TRACK OF YOUR PERSONAL PENSION PLANS

Name and address of plan provider and intermediary used (and date last checked)	Policy number	Date plan started	Date plan stopped	Last address you gave plan provided
Goldcrock Insurance plc 35-37 Money Road London EC4 18 7 88 Help Mates (Brokers) 25 Shackle Street London NW4	GI/105-3	18·7·88		26 Ogilvy St. Wembley Middlesex

The record sheet tells you:

Name and address of plan provider and financial adviser used, and date last checked: check and update this from time to time. Even if you don't expect to have further contact with an intermediary who set up the plan still keep a record of his details. This is in case you have a cause for complaint against him that only comes to light some time later

Policy number: the number you should quote when you contact the company, which will help them quickly to trace your details

Date plan started and stopped: useful information in any correspondence with the provider

Last address you gave the provider: make sure you give the plan provider your new address every time you move.

If an entry becomes out of date, cross it out and replace with the updated information. If you can't find the details of a plan, or have lost touch with the provider, track them down now – don't wait until retirement.

4

You can check whether the plan provider and/or financial adviser that you plan to use is an authorised business by looking them up in the Register kept (and updated daily) by the Securities and Investments Board (SIB) which oversees the workings of the Financial Services Act. The address is 3 Royal Exchange Buildings, London EC3V 3NL, telephone 01-929 3652. You can also check the register using Prestel, which is now available in most main libraries. If you come across a firm which does not seem to be authorised, do not do any business with it and alert SIB either at the above address or on this phone number: 01-283 2474.

If you have a complaint against an investment business, you should first contact the business itself, and take your compaint to the highest level, if necessary. If that is not successful, you can contact the organisation which authorised the firm for investment business. It will be one of the Self Regulating Organisations (SROs) or Recognised Professional Bodies (RPBs) listed right. Or in some cases, it will be the Securities and Investments Board itself (literature from the business will tell you who is the relevant SRO or RPB, or you can check the SIB Register). The addresses and telephone numbers of the SROs and RPBs relevant to personal pension plans are:

SIB
Securities and Investments Board,
3 Royal Exchange Buildings,
London EC3V 3NL.
Tel: 01-283 2474

Self Regulating Organisations
The Financial Intermediaries, Managers and Brokers Regulatory Association (FIMBRA), Hertsmere House, Marsh Wall, London E14 9RW.
Tel: 01-538 8860

Investment Management Regulatory Organisation (IMRO), Centre Point, 103 New Oxford Street, London WC1A 1QH.
Tel: 01-379 0601

Life Assurance and Unit Trust Regulatory Organisation (LAUTRO), Centre Point, 103 New Oxford Street, London WC1A 1QH.
Tel: 01-379 0444

Recognised Professional Bodies
Chartered Association of Certified Accountants, 29 Lincoln's Inn Fields, London WC2A 3EE.
Tel: 01-242 6855

Institute of Actuaries, Staple Inn Hall, High Holborn, London WC1V 7QJ.
Tel: 01-242 0106

Institute of Chartered Accountants in England and Wales, PO Box 433, Chartered Accountants' Hall, Moorgate Place, London EC2P 2BJ.
Tel: 01-628 7060

Institute of Chartered Accountants in Ireland, Chartered Accountants House, 87-89 Pembroke Road, Dublin 4.
Tel: 0001 680400

Institute of Chartered Accountants of Scotland, 27 Queen Street, Edinburgh EH2 1LA.
Tel: 031-255 5673

The Insurance Brokers Registration Council, 15 St Helen's Place, London EC3A 6DS.
Tel: 01-588 4387

The Law Society, 113 Chancery Lane, London WC2A 1PL.
Tel: 01-242 1222

Law Society of Northern Ireland, Law Society House, 90-106 Victoria Street, Belfast BT1 3JZ.
Tel: 0232 231614

Law Society of Scotland, Law Society Hall, 26 Drumsheugh Gardens, Edinburgh EH3 7YR.
Tel: 031-266 7411

If your complaint involves an insurance company or unit trust, it might be referred by the SRO to the Insurance Ombudsman or the Unit Trust Ombudsman if the company belongs to the scheme. If your complaint involves an adviser which is a member of FIMBRA, or falls within the aegis of IMRO, it may be referred to the Investment Referee.

If you have a complaint concerning deposit-based personal pension plans offered by banks or building societies, first contact the bank or building society taking your complaint to the highest level if necessary. If that is unsuccessful, you could contact the relevant Ombudsman:

The Banking Ombudsman, Citadel House, 5-11 Fetter Lane, London EC4A 1BR. Tel: 01-583 1395

The Building Societies Ombudsman, Grosvenor Gardens House, 35-37 Grosvenor Gardens, London SW1X 7AW. Tel: 01-931 0044

For a fee, you can get independent advice about the full range of your pension choices from a member of:

Society of Pension Consultants, Ludgate House, Ludgate Circus, London EC4A 2AB,

or

Association of Consulting Actuaries, Rolls House, Rolls Lane, Fetter Lane, London EC4A 1NH.

Both organisations can provide you with a list of members.

4

GLOSSARY OF PENSIONSPEAK

ADDITIONAL PENSION
Another name for pension from the State Earnings Related Pension Scheme (SERPS).

ADDITIONAL VOLUNTARY CONTRIBUTIONS
Extra contributions you choose to make to an employer's pension scheme to boost the pension and other benefits you'll get from the scheme.

ANNUITY
A regular income – for example paid monthly – which you get in exchange for a lump sum. 'Permanent' annuities provide an income for the rest of your life.

ANNUITY RATE
The amount of income you get when you buy an annuity, expressed as a proportion of the lump sum you invest.

APPROPRIATE PERSONAL PENSION
Personal pension plan which can be used to contract out of SERPS.

AVC
Abbreviation for Additional Voluntary Contribution.

BASIC PENSION
The flat-rate state pension paid to anyone (employed or self-employed) who has paid enough National Insurance contributions. If you don't have enough National Insurance contributions to qualify for the full rate, you might qualify for a pension at a reduced rate.

BENEFITS
What you get out of a pension scheme or plan – may include retirement pension, lump sum at retirement, widow's and widower's pensions, other dependants' pensions, pensions on retirement through ill health, increases to pensions, and lump sum life insurance.

CLASS 1 CONTRIBUTIONS
National Insurance contributions paid by employees and their employers. They count towards the full range of contributory state benefits.

CLASS 2 CONTRIBUTIONS
National Insurance contributions paid by the self-employed. Some contributory state benefits, namely sick pay, maternity pay, unemployment benefit and SERPS pension, aren't paid to the self-employed.

CLASS 3 CONTRIBUTIONS
National Insurance contributions that you can choose to pay to fill gaps in your contributions record for state basic pension (and widows' benefits).

CLASS 4 CONTRIBUTIONS
National Insurance contributions paid by the self-employed – but they don't entitle you to any benefits.

COMMUTATION
Exchanging part of your pension at retirement for a tax-free lump sum, subject to Inland Revenue rules.

COMPS
Abbreviation for Contracted Out Money Purchase Scheme.

CONTRACTED OUT MONEY PURCHASE SCHEME
An employer's money purchase pension scheme which will pay you a pension at state pension age, and other benefits, at least part of which is instead of SERPS benefits you would otherwise have got.

CONTRACTING OUT
Giving up part of your SERPS pension for a pension, and other benefits, from an employer's pension scheme or personal pension plan.

CONTRIBUTIONS

What your employer, you, and sometimes the Government too pay into a pension scheme or plan. Contributions to the state schemes are called National Insurance contributions.

DEFERRED PENSION

The pension you'll receive at retirement from a scheme to which contributions are no longer being paid.

DEPOSIT ADMINISTRATION SCHEME

Type of pension plan or fund provided by many insurance companies in which your contributions grow by having interest added. Once added, the interest can't be taken away (though rates can change).

DEPOSIT-BASED SCHEME

Type of pension plan offered by banks and building societies in which your contributions grow by having interest added. Once added the interest can't be taken away (though rates can change).

DEPARTMENT OF SOCIAL SECURITY

The Government department dealing with state pensions, among other matters.

DHSS

Abbreviation for Department of Health and Social Security – an old Government department which covered state pensions, among other matters.

DSS

Abbreviation for Department of Social Security.

EMPLOYER'S PENSION SCHEME

Scheme run by an employer to provide employees with a pension at retirement and, usually, other benefits as well.

FINAL PAY SCHEME

Type of pension scheme in which pension, and some other benefits, are related to your pay near retirement (or when you leave the scheme) and the number of years for which you've been a member of the scheme.

FREE STANDING ADDITIONAL VOLUNTARY CONTRIBUTIONS

Contributions you choose to make to add to the pension and other benefits you get from an employer's pension scheme, which you pay into a scheme you select rather than your employer's scheme.

FSAVC

Abbreviation for Free Standing Additional Voluntary Contributions.

GMP

Abbreviation for Guaranteed Minimum Pension.

GRADUATED PENSION

Relatively small earnings-related pension from a state scheme, based on contributions made between 1961 and 1975.

GUARANTEED MINIMUM PENSION

The amount by which your SERPS pension is reduced if you are contracted out of SERPS. Also the minimum amount of pension you receive at retirement from a final pay scheme for periods when you were contracted out.

HOME RESPONSIBILITIES PROTECTION

Scheme to protect your entitlement to basic and SERPS pensions while you are caring for someone at home – for example, children or an elderly relative.

HYBRID SCHEMES

Pension schemes which work out pensions, and other benefits, on an alternative of final pay and money purchase bases, and give you whichever is the better.

INFLATION

Sustained increase in price or earnings levels, commonly measured by changes in the Retail Prices Index (price inflation) or changes in the Index of National Average Earnings (earnings inflation).

INLAND REVENUE

Government department dealing with, *inter alia,* income tax affairs.

LOWER EARNINGS LIMIT

Minimum level of earnings at which Class 1 National Insurance contributions start to be paid (by both employees and employers). Used in the calculation of entitlement to various benefits, it is set each year and is approximately equal to the state basic pension.

MAPP

Abbreviation for Minimum Appropriate Personal Pension.

MARRIED WOMEN'S REDUCED RATE CONTRIBUTIONS

Lower rate of Class 1 National Insurance contributions paid by some married women and widows. They opted for this lower rate before April 1977 in return for dropping any rights to state pensions.

MIDDLE BAND EARNINGS

Earnings between the Lower and Upper Earnings Limits for Class 1 National Insurance contributions.

MINIMUM APPROPRIATE PERSONAL PENSION

Personal pension plan used to contract out of SERPS. It accepts only the DSS rebate (and incentive, if applicable) and must be used solely to provide protected rights when the plan holder reaches state pension age.

MONEY PURCHASE SCHEME

Pension scheme or plan in which the eventual pension, and other benefits, depend on the amount contributed, how invested contributions grow, and annuity rates at the time of retirement.

NATIONAL INSURANCE

A state insurance scheme which provides pensions and other benefits in return for contribution payments.

NATIONAL INSURANCE CREDITS

Class 1 or Class 3 contributions added to your record, at times when you cannot pay them. You are entitled to credits only in specified circumstances, such as sickness, unemployment, training and pregnancy.

NI REBATE

The part of your and your employer's National Insurance contributions which the DSS pays to a personal pension plan to provide 'protected rights' if you contract out of SERPS. Also the amount by which NI contributions are reduced if you are contracted out through an employer's scheme, and the amount which must be paid into a contracted out money purchase scheme.

OCCUPATIONAL PENSION SCHEME

Another name for an employer's pension scheme.

PENSION

Regular income, usually paid for life.

PERSONAL PENSION PLAN

A pension scheme you arrange for yourself with an insurance company, friendly society, unit trust, building society or bank. It will provide you with a pension at retirement, and possibly other benefits, according to the amount you have contributed, how invested contributions grow and annuity rates at the time of retirement. Not connected with a specific job or career, so sometimes called a portable pension.

PPP

Abbreviation for a personal pension plan.

PROTECTED RIGHTS

The benefits which you get from a contracted out money purchase employer's scheme or contracted out (appropriate) personal pension plan in place of SERPS pension you give up. They are a retirement pension which must increase by up to 3% a year, and a widow's or widower's pension.

RETAIL PRICES INDEX

Government measure of the average price level in the UK. Changes in the Index are commonly used as a measure of price inflation.

RETIREMENT PENSIONS FORECASTING AND ADVICE SERVICE

Government computerised service for telling you what is your current, and possible future, entitlement to state pensions.

RPI

Abbreviation for Retail Prices Index.

SECTION 32 PLAN

Specialppension plan you can take out to provide a pension in return for you investing the transfer value you get from an employer's pension scheme or personal pension plan which you have left. Also called 'Buy out' plans.

SECTION 226 PLAN

Old-style personal pension plan superceded from 1 July 1988 by personal pension plans. Can't be used for contracting out of SERPS.

SERPS

Abbreviation for State Earnings Related Pension Scheme.

STATE EARNINGS RELATED PENSION SCHEME

The state pension scheme which pays a pension related to your earnings since 1978. If you work for an employer, you can contract out of this part of the state scheme.

STATE PENSION AGE

The earliest age at which you can start to receive state retirement pensions – 65 for men and 60 for women

TRANSFER VALUE

Amount of money you would have to invest now to provide the pension, and any other benefits, that you are entitled to from a pension scheme you are leaving or a personal plan you are stopping. The transfer value is paid into another plan or scheme, subject to some restrictions in respect of GMP and protected rights.

UNITISED WITH-PROFITS PLAN

Fund within a unit-linked pension plan which works in a similar way to a with-profits plan. The amount in the fund rises as units are revalued and bonus units added, and can't fall.

UNIT-LINKED PLAN

Pension plan offered by many insurance companies in which the value of your invested contributions is linked to a specific fund of investments. The value of your plan can go down as well as up.

UNIT TRUST PLAN

Pension plan offered by some unit trusts in which contributions are used to buy a stake (in the form of a number of 'units') in a specific pool of investments. The value of your plan depends on the performance of the underlying investments, and can go down as well as up.

UPPER EARNINGS LIMIT

Maximum level of earnings on which employees pay Class 1 National Insurance contributions (there is no upper limit for employers). Used in the calculation of entitlement to SERPS pension, it is set each year.

WITH-PROFITS PLAN

Pension plan provided by insurance companies. The return on contributions depends on the performance of the insurance company, reflecting factors such as investment performance, expenses, profit-distribution policy and so on. Your return is in the form of bonuses which are added to your plan at intervals, and when the plan comes to an end. Once added, bonuses can't be taken away.

WORKING LIFE

Maximum number of years you could work up to state retirement age (as officially defined), used to calculate your entitlement to basic pension. For most people it means the tax years from age 16 to just before reaching state pension age – usually 44 years for a woman, and 49 years for a man.

OTHER PACKS AVAILABLE IN THIS SERIES

MAKE YOUR WILL £6.95

Making a will is an essential step for anyone with responsibilities, it should be updated regularly; especially when your circumstances change – for example, you get married, have children or divorce. Inside the pack you will find three different types of will form and careful guidance on working out what you want in your will. The pack is based on the law as it applies in England and Wales and is not suitable for people based in Scotland or Northern Ireland.

Available from bookshops or from:

Consumers' Association
PO Box 44
Hertford SG14 1SH

FINANCE YOUR FUTURE £6.95

A practical guide to financial security in retirement. The younger you are when you take stock and plan your finances, the more likely you are to enjoy a comfortable and worry-free retirement. This pack takes you through six practical steps using budget forms, ready reckoners, a unique pensions and savings calculator and a set of fact sheets. An essential tool for that mid-life review!

Credit card holders can ring their order FREE to Consumers' Association on 0800-252100 quoting their Access or Visa card number.